VIPASSANA MINDFULNESS

An Introduction to the Practice of Vipassana Meditation

~ by Chaya Rao ~

Table of Contents

Introduction 1

Chapter 1: What is Vipassana? 7

Chapter 2: Preliminary Preparations 11

Chapter 3: Sitting Vipassana (the First Exercise)...................17

Chapter 4: Labelling...19

Chapter 5: Observing Motion 23

Chapter 6: Observing Sensation 25

Chapter 7: If You ABSOLUTELY Have to Move 29

Chapter 8: A Few Warnings 31

Chapter 9: Active Vipassana..35

Conclusion..39

Introduction

The correct way to pronounce it is *vih-PUS sun-NAA* — stress on the second and last syllables. It comes from Pali (which is to Theravada Buddhists what Latin is to Roman Catholics) and can mean "insight", "clear-seeing", or "seeing very deeply."

You don't have to be a Buddhist to practice Vipassana. A growing number of scientists, doctors, atheists, convicts, and many others are taking it up.

Why convicts? Well, they were the ones who actually showed the benefits of Vipassana to the western world, in a way. Practiced throughout Asia for thousands of years, it remained there until the late 20th century when people like Ledi Sayadaw and Satya Narayan Goenka took it out of its monastic settings.

Thanks to their efforts, Vipassana reached the western world, but remained almost exclusively within Asian communities — but not for long. The 1960s had introduced westerners to Asian ideas and influences, while mass media did the rest.

In 1975, Vipassana was taught at a prison in Jaipur, India, surprising everyone with its success in rehabilitating hardened criminals. Impressed with the outcome, Tihar Jail, India's largest penitentiary, decided to follow suit with similar success. The result was the award-winning documentary, "Doing Time, Doing Vipassana."

The first American prison to experiment with Vipassana was the North Rehabilitation Facility in Seattle, Washington in 1997. Despite much scepticism, it too, was a success, resulting in another famous documentary called "The Dhamma Brothers." Since then, the number of American jails which have a Vipassana program has grown.

Vipassana is a form of meditation, a mental exercise, if you will. It's not a belief system, religion, or a philosophy. Though Buddhist in origin, it isn't dependent on Buddhism, as Sayadaw, Goenka, and others proved. This is why a growing number of non-Buddhists have begun learning it without fear of compromising their religious beliefs.

Medical research has proven that meditation affects people in positive ways. It can relieve stress, anxiety, depression, reduce blood pressure, end drug dependency, and help with pain management — greatly minimizing the need for medication. It's also effective in dealing with anger management issues, post traumatic stress, and hormonal changes (those that are seasonal or even from drug use).

Studies have also shown that meditation improves productivity in the work place. It heightens memory, concentration, and focus, and helps those with cognitive difficulties. The best thing of all is that meditation practice, be it Vipassana or some other discipline, requires no investment and no special equipment.

This book will delve into Vipassana, explaining everything you need to know to practice Vipassana regularly in your life so that you can reap all its benefits, including getting rid of all your stress and instead live full of happiness, peace, and joy.

Chapter 1: What is Vipassana?

Vipassana is a breathing and concentration technique which focuses on teaching us mindfulness.

The Buddha taught that a major reason why people suffer is because they tend to be mindless. Have you ever gone to the kitchen to get something, only to forget what it was you wanted as soon as you got there? That's mindlessness.

You probably wanted a glass of water. Between that thought and the kitchen, however, so many other things entered your mind that your original intent (to get a glass of water) got squeezed out.

While that example was harmless, imagine driving on the highway while being mindless, or having a doctor operate on you while his or her mind is millions of miles away.

Mindlessness is cumulative and manifests itself in every part of our lives, affecting our moods, our performance, and our relationships with others and ourselves. In many cases, mindlessness can even affect our health.

The Buddha believed that the reason people become mindless is because they tend to live in an automatic mode. People don't generally like challenges, preferring the simple over the complex and the easy over the difficult. Thinking things through is both challenging and complex, so most avoid it if given a choice.

People also prefer instant rewards. If something feels good they go for it, regardless of the consequences. Even when they realize that something is bad for them they can't stop because they're stuck in automatic.

You know smoking is bad for you, for example, but because you're addicted to nicotine, you just can't stop. Different things become addicting for different reasons but they're all the result of mindlessness, the ease of habit, and the desire for instant gratification.

This is why we tend to get stuck in the same dead end job, the same toxic relationships, and the same rut. We may hate it, but it's a routine, and there's something comforting about routines, even if we end up regretting the result.

Vipassana doesn't require you to wear robes, chant, grow your hair or shave it, become a vegetarian, follow a guru, or believe in god, the afterlife, or anything like that.

To know that you have certain habits, good or bad, is one thing. To find environmental, psychological, social, political, and economic reasons for them, is another. Vipassana looks at none of these.

Rather, it looks to the mind and body on the basis that what affects one affects the other. It is not concerned with reasons, or how you related to your parents as a child. It is focused solely on your thoughts and feelings in the here and now.

This form of meditation strives to break us out of our mental rut by treating the mind, and one's state of mind, in the same way that a body builder treats his or her muscles.

The idea behind Vipassana is that mindfulness is an inherent quality that we can develop with regular and consistent practice. The more we pay attention to how our minds work, the more control we have over it. And the more control we have over our minds, the more control we have over our own bodies and our lives.

It isn't easy breaking out of automatic mode, though. It takes a lot of time, patience, and practice — just ask any athlete or body builder. You don't honestly think those people were born with such fantastic abilities and bodies, do you?

But if you're no longer happy with the way things are going for you, or even if you are but want more out of your life, then it's time to start paying attention to yourself.

So how do you practice Vipassana? There are basically two ways.

Without getting into tongue-tying Pali syllables, we can simply call them:

1) Sitting Vipassana, and

2) Active Vipassana

Chapter 2: Preliminary Preparations

Before any exercise, there are certain things you should do in order to enjoy a successful session. You don't work out at the gym, jog, or play a sport without first setting aside a few minutes for a proper warm-up to get your body ready, right?

Think of the following as your warm-up for Vipassana, a workout for the mind.

1) Location

While Vipassana can be done anywhere, it's best to pick a spot where you won't be disturbed for at least ten to fifteen minutes. Advanced practitioners can even do it in a busy and noisy office, but if you're reading this, you're probably not there yet.

Treat your Vipassana practice as you would a gym session. If your workout keeps getting interrupted, it does you no good. If you live with others, lock your door or post a "DO NOT DISTURB" sign during your session.

2) Clothes

Remove your shoes and wear comfortable, loose clothing. If your pants or belt are tight, loosen them. Your body temperature tends to rise when you do sitting meditation, so if you're wearing very warm clothing, bear that in mind.

3) Resolution

This is optional. If ten minutes is all you can spare for a session, then make a vow to see those ten minutes through. You don't have to swear on a holy book, just tell yourself that you won't get up halfway through — and keep your word.

Have a watch nearby to make sure you don't fall short of your goal. You can set an alarm, but avoid one that's too loud and jarring. It would also help to shut off your phone and visit the bathroom before you settle down, to make sure you fulfil your resolution.

Regular practitioners make their sessions a daily habit. For best results, it's also advisable to stick to the same time each day. This conditions your body and mind to get into the right mood.

4) Sitting

Whether you sit for ten minutes or more, it's important to keep still. If you're comfortable sitting cross-legged on the floor without shifting or fidgeting, then more power to you.

If this is the route you want to take, make sure your cushion is especially thick. Thin cushions will flatten when you sit on them long enough, which can cause discomfort as your backside presses against the floor.

A cushion that's big enough to accommodate your crossed legs is best. Given enough time, the top ankle pressing on the bottom one causes it to fall asleep as blood circulation gets cut off. A very thick cushion will solve this problem.

If you'd prefer to sit on a chair, make sure it's one without a back. A stool would be best, but if you don't have one of those, avoid touching the back of your chair with.... well, your back. The way your body shifts and adjusts during a session is important, but we'll get into that later.

Make sure your feet are both firmly on the floor, not crossed at the ankles or with one leg resting on the other. Since you have to keep still, this is a great way to avoid cramps and other discomfort.

Avoid sitting on a couch. They're designed to make you lean backward, which is not good for a session as you might nod off. Also avoid slouching forward for the same reason. When you slouch, you contract your stomach and chest, decreasing your oxygen intake which can make you sleepy or tired.

Place your hands on your lap. Find a position that will allow them to remain in place comfortably without effort on your part. Some clasp their fingers together, while others rest their hands before their groin with one hand palm up and the other resting on it, also palm up. There is no right or wrong here, only what works best for you.

Fidget all you like until you find a position you're sure you can hold comfortably throughout the entire session. Be sure your back is ramrod straight and that your shoulders are pulled back comfortably so you can breathe easily.

Your head should not fall forward so your chin rests against your neck. Look straight ahead so the underside of your jaw lies parallel to the floor. Keep your lips closed and let your jaw sag slightly so there's a gap between your upper and lower teeth.

5) Breathing

For many people, this is one of the trickiest parts.

Babies and toddlers breathe naturally: with their stomachs. This is the healthiest and most efficient way, as it maximizes our oxygen intake and carbon dioxide outtake. As we grow older, however, we start breathing through our chests, which is unhealthy as it contributes to stress and a host of other diseases.

Practice breathing by relaxing your shoulders and chest, letting your in-breath go straight down into your stomach. When you exhale, push out with your stomach only.

If you watch yourself in a mirror, you'll see that it's not as easy as it sounds, but with practice, you'll get it eventually. You'll know you're successful when your shoulders and chest no longer move as you breathe in and out.

Chapter 3: Sitting Vipassana (the First Exercise)

Close your eyes.

Focus your attention on your abdomen a few inches above your belly button, at the point where your stomach makes a crease when you bend forward. This is your body's midpoint.

If you pay attention to your breathing, there's a bit of pressure here at the end of each inhalation and exhalation; regardless of whether you have a six pack of abs or a spare tire. You must not visualize this point, but feel it with your body. If it helps, touch your midpoint with your finger so you know where it is without having to visualize it.

Whenever you breathe in, your abdomen expands. This is called "rising." Whenever you exhale, your abdomen contracts, which is "falling".

After each in-breath and out-breath is a pause called "stillness," which produces two different sensations. The stillness after each in-breath provides a feeling of fullness and tension, while the one after each out-breath makes you feel relaxed.

There is a tendency to lean back when you inhale and to lean forward when you exhale, so keep your back slightly arched to keep yourself stable. Again, avoid resting your back against something for reasons that will be explained later.

Your goal is to keep your focus on your breathing at your body's midpoint. Every time thoughts come in, or your attention wanders away, firmly bring your mind back to each in-breath and out-breath.

Forget about the next several seconds or minutes, and don't let images or distractions enter your mind. Whenever they intrude, simply bring your mind back to your breathing.

How simple is that? Actually, it isn't simple. Fortunately, there are ways of dealing with this.

Chapter 4: Labelling

It shouldn't take you long to realize that your mind is engaged in constant dialogue. You see things, people, and events, but your mind never really lets you just relax and observe. Your mind has to make a comment about everything, and if you let it go on long enough, you eventually find yourself in parts unknown.

If you witness a fender-bender, for example, your eyes tell you that two or more cars just collided. Your mind, on the other hand has to have its say:

"Ooh! What an idiot, how did that other driver not see that coming?! I'm glad I don't drive like that. I'm sure I have my insurance updated, but I'd better check just to be safe. And on that subject, I wonder if my last check went through. I have to pay my phone bill, which stresses me out because it's too expensive but I'm stuck on that two-year plan. I wonder where I'll be in two years, and..."

You're no longer there. You're off on a completely different tangent.

The aim of Vipassana is to train your mind to go quiet, even if only for ten minutes. You want your mind to stay focused in the here and now, not think about the past, comment about the present, or wonder about the future.

Unfortunately, you've let it have its say for so long that your mind has developed a mind of its own. Think of your mind as a hyperactive puppy. Even if you take it to the best dog obedience school, you won't see results overnight. It takes a while, so you have to condition it gradually.

Labelling is a useful technique that allows your mind to get a grip on a specific thought or feeling without letting it get off tangent.

As you breathe in, think "rising." As you breathe out, think "falling." While there is "stillness" after each inhalation and exhalation, you can dispense with it. You want to minimize labelling to avoid the temptation of internal dialogue.

Every time you think thoughts like "this is such a waste of time," "I wonder if I'm doing this right," or "I hope no one comes in and sees me," cut that commentary off by labelling each process as "thinking."

Make sure you use only one word for your labelling and not a phrase or a sentence. If you hear a car honking, don't label it as "car horn, off in distance on the street, probably the mailman." Use "hearing" instead. If your ankle starts itching or your shoulder starts cramping, don't describe them. Simply use "itching" or "pain," respectively.

If a sensation or sound arises that you don't know how to label, simply use "knowing" or "feeling." If the thought, emotion, or image becomes intense and fights for attention, simply repeat your label until it passes.

Do not do forced or wishful labelling. Some people find certain thoughts hard to get rid of, so they think something like "letting that thought go now... going... going... I SAID GOING! GET OUT OF HERE!"

This not only causes frustration and encourages further mental dialogue, it's also self-defeating. Labelling must only be done whenever a thought, feeling, image, or sensation arises. It must never be used to influence an outcome.

Above all, there must be no emotional attachment to labels. "Thinking," "feeling," "knowing," etc., were chosen because they are deliberately devoid of emotion and moral judgment.

It is irrelevant if the thought, image, or feeling is good or bad. The point of this first exercise is to make you aware of just how much internal dialogue you engage in. The fact that you become aware of it is a success in itself, so there's no need to be hard on yourself.

Vipassana is not about self-judgment. Neither is it about introspection. Vipassana simply helps to make us aware of what's going on inside.

Think of your distracting thoughts, emotions, and feelings as a movie on a screen with a life of its own. Every time a movie plays, you lose a point. Every time you succeed in pressing the "off" button, you score a point. But whenever you react emotionally to a failure, you lose several points.

You can also think of this as a game. Your goal is to keep focused on your breathing. Each thought that arises is a point against you, and the longer you entertain that thought, the more points you lose. Labelling is the weapon you use to destroy that thought and get your focus back on your breathing.

With regular practice, your internal dialogue should start to decrease to the point that you can do without labelling. Your objective is to simply feel each rising, stillness, and falling without any mental commentary whatsoever.

Chapter 5: Observing Motion

Only statues and corpses can keep absolutely still. Even when lying down, we're never still, thanks to our need to breathe. Although your breathing occurs in three stages, there is far more going on that you should be paying attention to. The more closely you can focus on these things, the less chance your mind has of engaging in a monologue.

As you take a breath into your stomach, pay close attention to how your stomach slowly tenses up and expands. This is followed by the pause, the exhalation, and your stomach contracting. Your goal is to keep up an even, steady rhythm with no emotional attachment to any process whatsoever.

You may have issues with your body but you can deal with that after the session. For the moment, observe your breathing and the sensations that come with it as closely as you can.

While your main focus should be on your breath, you should also be aware of what's happening with the rest of your body. When you sit up, your body constantly makes tiny adjustments in order to keep you upright.

Fortunately, this need to maintain balance is a valuable tool in Vipassana, and explains why you should avoid a back support.

There is a temptation, especially in the beginning, to feel so relaxed that you fall asleep. Making sure you remain upright, with the underside of your jaw parallel to the floor and your lips closed while your jaw sags comfortably, should keep you awake.

If you find yourself leaning forward too much, or to one side or the other, make the necessary adjustment to avoid falling over. This constant need to maintain balance, as well as your constant focus on what's happening to your body, will hopefully keep you centered in the present.

Chapter 6: Observing Sensation

This one is quite difficult. Remember how you're supposed to keep still throughout the entire session? In Vipassana, this means that the only movement you're allowed to do is the bare minimum required to breathe and to keep your body upright.

Even if you feel an itch, a cramp, or something else, you keep still, no matter what. No scratching, no stretching, no fidgeting — period. If you're alone, you can get away with this, but during a group session, those teachers and their assistants keep a beady eye out for violators.

The truth is that we feel all manner of discomforts, such as itching, several times a day. However, we're often too distracted to notice them.

Have you ever cut yourself and felt nothing for several minutes until you saw the bleeding? It was only when you finally noticed it that the pain came. That's because your mind was too busy on something else to tell you about the damage and the pain.

Even if we keep ourselves clean, our bodies itch several times in a single hour, but we rarely notice it because our minds are far away. Often, we do scratch, but we do so mindlessly, so we forget that we did.

During a Vipassana session, with fewer distractions, you will most certainly notice those itches. But you're still not allowed to scratch.

These sensations, you see, are considered to be valuable tools. Vipassana's ultimate objective is to strengthen the mind so that it is in control of the body, not the other way around. Its other goal is to show that nothing is permanent.

When an itch arises, ignore it by keeping your focus on your breath. If it's a minor one, it should go away, as most itches that we don't notice eventually do. If it's a major one, then label it "itching."

Your job, at this point, is to maintain an emotional distance from the sensation. Rather than going on automatic and scratching it unthinkingly, pay attention to the itch.

Is it intense or mild? Does it throb or does it sort of pulsate? Where on the body is it? How far from the epicentre does it extend? Does it stop itching past a certain point, and if so, at what point? Is there an in-between part where the itch is strongest and where it seems weakest?

This detached observation of the sensation will take your attention away from the breath, it is true, but this distraction is acceptable and part of the session. You will notice that the itch does indeed go away without the need to scratch, and when it does, simply bring your attention back to your breathing.

Do not think, "Whew! I got past that hurdle! Now, back to the rising and falling...".

This is dialogue. Worse, it is an emotional one. Whatever happens, simply focus on your breathing. If an itch distracts you too much, label it, observe it dispassionately until it passes, then return to your rising and falling.

Chapter 7: If You ABSOLUTELY Have to Move

Fortunately, Vipassana teachers and their assistants are not unreasonable. If an itch is driving you up the wall despite your best efforts (perhaps because a mosquito bit you), then do the following:

a. Notice your intense desire to scratch and label it "desire." If that itch is still bugging you and you REALLY have to scratch, focus on your hand.

b. Before you move it, label the thought as "intending."

c. Slowly move your hand to the spot, and label it as "moving."

d. Hover your hand over the itchy spot but don't scratch. Use "intending" once more before you actually scratch.

e. When you finally get to it, label your action as "moving" or "scratching." Do not use "gratitude" because that's emotional.

f. When the itch finally passes, use "stop" when you finish scratching, "moving" when you return your hand to its original position, and "placing" as you settle it back down.

g. You may take a few seconds to note the relieved feeling, but avoid using emotional labels like "liking." "Pleasant" or "relieved" would be best.

h. Now return your focus to your breathing.

While this exercise may sound strange, the point is to develop sensitivity to how your mind works *while it is working*. Though exaggerated, it also aims to break you out of automatic mode by being aware of each thought as it arises, as well as the actions which follow each thought.

When dealing with cramps, pain, or anything else that requires you to shift or to fidget, do not react immediately. Focus on your breathing or label it until it passes. But if it doesn't, then follow the above steps.

Chapter 8: A Few Warnings

While Vipassana is a safe and healthy exercise, there are a few things to watch out for.

Dizziness or Light-headedness

Some people feel dizzy or nauseous when they first do the breathing exercise. This has nothing to do with meditation, but with the fact that they've probably been breathing from their chests for far too long. The sudden intake of more oxygen than they are used to is responsible for such discomfort.

To compensate, simply take smaller and shallower breaths — but do so with your stomach, not your chest. With enough practice, you can take deeper and longer breaths without feeling discomfort.

Visions

There's a famous story about a student of the Buddha who got up from a meditation session and began jumping up and down with joy. The man claimed that an angel appeared to him and showered him with divine love.

The Buddha calmly opened his eyes, smiled at the man, and said, "That's nice. Focus on your breathing and it'll go away."

Scientists are beginning to understand that people who see visions are not necessarily crazy. It's just that there's a lot of stuff going on in our brains and bodies that can make us see things that aren't really there. Sometimes, oxygen intake is responsible, evidenced by the number of divers and surgery patients who experience hallucinations.

Whatever the case, the Buddha's suggestion is as valid today as it was when he first uttered it. If you do hallucinate, don't panic, start a new religion, or give all your stuff away. It's probably those leftovers you had before your session.

Simply focus on your breathing. If it takes a while to go away, simply label it "image" till it does.

Pain

Some people are extremely competitive. When told they can't move until after a session (unless they become too uncomfortable), they treat it as a competition and refuse to move no matter what.

This is not wise. Pain is your body's way of telling you there's damage. Refusing to move to alleviate intense pain or cramping is asking for trouble. While you should follow the steps outlined in the previous section, you should also follow your body's wisdom and be adaptable.

Chapter 9: Active Vipassana

This covers a wide field, but since this is only an introduction, we'll cover walking and daily practice. Remember how in chapter one, we talked about going to the kitchen to get a glass of water, only to forget what you wanted as soon as you got to the kitchen? The next time you do that, do it the Vipassana way.

Use labels for the following, which we'll leave out for brevity's sake.

Pay attention to how your body feels as you get up from your chair. Do your knees hurt? Is there strain on your hips? Do you have to push up with your arms and hands? Notice how your legs and feet feel as they propel you toward the kitchen. If you're wearing shoes, focus on any sound they make as they touch the floor and to how your feet widen as they press down.

Once in the kitchen, what do you smell? What's the temperature and quality of the light like? How does your arm feel as it reaches out for a glass? Observe your hand as your fingers wrap around that glass, as well as to the feel of that glass — its weight, texture, and temperature.

Pay attention to the act of pouring, to the sound of the water falling, and to the feel of the changing weight and temperature of the glass as it fills up. Notice how your arm crooks at the elbow as you lift that glass, and to the way your wrist bends as you tilt it toward your mouth.

How does the glass feel as it presses against your lips and teeth? And the water as it floods your mouth? How about your throat as the water pours down it?

Get the idea? In some Vipassana classes, it can take as long as an hour to drink a simple cup of tea!

Walking and daily practice are the same things. It's simply paying attention to what you do as you do it, as well as to the sensations, sights, and sounds around you. Labelling helps in the beginning, but your ultimate goal is to do without it, to experience your own thoughts and actions as they occur without comment.

This is obviously not an easy thing to maintain, but with practice, you'll find yourself able to do it for longer periods.

Some find it easier to practice active Vipassana because the thought of sitting still, even for ten minutes, makes them impatient. They keep opening their eyes to look at the clock, not trusting their alarm to work. While both practices go hand-in-hand, start off with what feels best for you.

Conclusion

There is no magic to Vipassana. It's a deceptively simple exercise that requires no fanfare, only regular practice — but the long-term benefits are immense. There's also a lot more to it, but as an introduction, this will have to do.

If you'd like to know more, visit the Dhamma Organization (www.dhamma.org). They have several thousand Vipassana Meditation Centers throughout the world which offer free 10-day retreats. That "free" includes vegetarian food and lodging, by the way, funded by donations and staffed by volunteers.

There are other Vipassana groups out there, and while their approaches vary, the outline given in the previous chapters remains the core. Moving beyond medical studies regarding stress relief and whatnot, the Buddha taught that mental training is key to becoming a better human being.

He said that, "We are shaped by our thoughts; we become what we think. When the mind is pure, joy follows like a shadow that never leaves."

Vipassana teaches us that happiness is not dependent on something out there that comes and goes. If we can develop a calm and disciplined mind, happiness will remain forever within us, instead.

May you therefore learn to always be mindful and thus happy.

Last, I'd like to thank you for purchasing this book! If you enjoyed it or found it helpful, I'd greatly appreciate it if you'd take a moment to leave a review on Amazon. Thank you!

Also, please consider checking my other books, also available on Amazon:

- **Buddhist Beliefs & Principles**: Understanding the Basic Principles of Buddhism and How to Incorporate Buddhism into Your Life ~ Buddhism for Beginners

  by Chaya Rao

- **Dharma and Dhamma** ~ An Overview of Dharma and Dhamma, and How to Apply them in Daily Life (includes Moksha, the Four Noble Truths, the Eightfold Path, and Nibanna)

  by Chaya Rao

Made in the USA
Las Vegas, NV
30 October 2022

58428284R00026